WYRESDALE
in Times Past

Scorton
Dolphinholme
Abbeystead

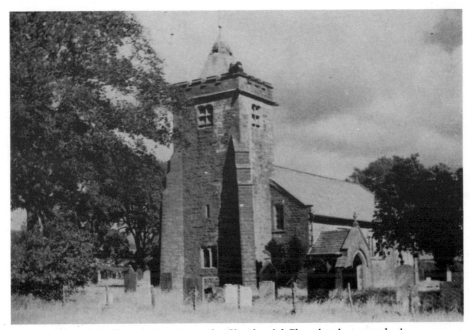

Wyresdale Church, known as the Shepherds' Church, photographed about 80 years ago.

Catherine Rothwell

Cover: An 1890s Congregational Sunday School outing of teachers at Dolphinholm{...} {...}ht is
E. le Mare, father of the late Noel le Mare, owner of the race horse Red Rum.

1

Acknowledgements

Mrs. Wendy Adam; Mrs. F. Anderton; Mr. and Mrs. F. G. Apedaile; R. C. Banks; A. J. Boorman; Stanley Butterworth; Margaret Collinson; Mr. J. Cross; Andrew Curwen; Mrs. T. Entwistle; The Grosvenor Estate, Abbeystead Estate; Rev. L. J. Hakes; Mrs. P. Hall; the late Noel Le Mare; Eric and Elaine Longton; North West Water Authority, Lancaster; The Priory Cafe, Scorton; Jack Pye; Mr. W. G. Richmond; Mrs. L. Ronson; E. G. Rothwell; Ron Severs; the late R. G. Shepherd; Mr. R. E. Smith; Jack Staziak; Mrs. Catherine Tallentire; Richard Tallentire; Wendy's Memory Lane; Arthur West; Frank Williams; Ruth Yates; Lancashire Record Office.

Introduction

Settlements in Wyresdale have a place in history going back further than the Norman Conquest. Small wonder then that so much information was brought to light in tracing the course of the River Wyre from its sources to the sea, more indeed than could be used in one small book—so it seemed a good idea to work on another and this time to concentrate on such interesting places as Scorton, Abbeystead, Dolphinholme and the reaches of Wyresdale. Hundreds of years ago the Forest of Wyresdale extended from the dale head at Tarnbrook to Pilling dykes and the Wyre estuary. Early hunters ranged the swampy, fertile coastal plain in winter to return to the foothills in summertime.

In the 13th. century Wyresdale was one large vaccary under that name. The English antiquary William Camden in the 1500s thought it a solitary, dismal place, to be approached like the Lake District with dread. The boundaries of the Forest were perambulated annually, Catshaw, Marshaw, Tarnbrook, Ward Stone and the watershed stone in the Trough of Bowland for the days of Border raids, when the Scots came down like wolves on the fold, were fresh in mind. In front of Marshaw Farm there is a hollow called The Stables where cattle were herded at such times and the church towers of Bowland, places of refuge, were strongly built, some six feet thick at their base.

A 1710 Gazetteer refers to Wiresdale, a small village in the Hundred of Lunesdale. Long known for its severe weather, January 10th. 1792 brought hailstones to Abbeystead six inches long and ice two inches thick. Fingers froze to door snecks, ink froze in horns and, worst of all, "the milk was frozen in the buttery".

Yet, in the summer of the same year, following drought, July witnessed "a great flood in Wyre, a cloudburst over Marshaw and the slate quarry at Tarnbrook", which resulted in tubs, butter basins, dishes and stools being washed down with trees. The Cawthorne Arms was flooded and the factory at Dolphinholme stood four feet deep in water.

Later historians modified descriptios of the dangerous wilderness, for Fenton Cawthorne, an early conservationist, brought great changes by improving the land. He desired more lush pasture like that towards Forton and Scorton and by 1821 The Lonsdale Magazine could voice: "All the scenery about Wyresdale is of an agreeable nature, rich old woods, fertile meadows, a fine river...the simple natives administer to each other's wants, labour to preserve and improve new farms, still treasure thatched cottages and the oaken furniture of their forefathers." Machinery had not taken over as it had in the towns; religion was more sincere, "not hypocritical or fanatical". The hired Overseer of the Poor in Nether Wyresdale two centuries ago had entries like this in his accounts:

delving and farming—8 days—10 shillings and 8 pence
Paper to make Militia List 2 pence
Moles—catching—15 shillings and 9 pence 3 farthings
Paid for eggs and birds £1-10-6½
Paid for waistcotts (waistcoats) 3 shillings

The appointment annually at Lancaster of ale-tasters, hedge lookers, leather sealers, flesh lookers, moormen, reflects the age when quaintness of tenure could charm. Amidst peppercorn rents Henrietta Harrison of the vaccary of Haythornthwaite was paid annually a quart of cranberries by eight of her tenants.

The old trades looked set to last for ever: wheelwright; blacksmith; gamekeeper; coachman; verderer; groom; travelling tailor. Harking back 900 years, the harsh tyranny of the Assize of the Forest died hard, poaching even in the 19th. century still being punished out of all proportion to the offence. Wild boar and wolves passed into history; foxes, hares, rabbits, martens, deer and otter were still at large. The 24 Sworn Men of Wyresdale paid Joshua Jackson for six foxes but a sore point was the office of Bowbearer or Master Forester, held by J. Fenton Cawthorne in 1825. The right to hunt over all land having been conferred, Captain Ormrod's pack of buck hounds and the Wyresdale Hunt trampled crops and broke fences. From time immemorial this inevitably caused trouble.

With the Cawthornes and the Garnetts came a tidying up (to this day, Wyresdale hedges are clipped and shaped when Royalty is expected at Abbeystead House). Derelict farms and barns had their valuable stone carted off for fresh building. Threap Hall, above Tower Lodge, was so named because of the grumbling of the brothers who tried unsuccessfully to farm it. When the homestead fell about their ears the neighbours reckoned it was a judgment upon them.

Given the atmosphere and wealth of ancient country lore, one would expect ghosts and witches. The old house at Lower Lea, Hathornthwaite, was haunted by Old Gorst or Goose, whilst Old Anthony's more sprightly ghost at Dunkenshaw was often seen jumping over the garden wall on summer nights. He had reputedly been buried in the garden instead of the churchyard. It was through the Trough of Bowland and on to Lancaster that Demdike, Chattox and gruesome companions trailed to trial and execution.

Many stories were told of Mr. Fenton Cawthorne's bold ventures and generosity. Whilst he was dining with friends at his shooting lodge, Wyresdale Tower, word was quietly brought to him at table that the bailiffs had arrived. "Pocket the silver and slip away," was his plea to the startled guests. As debts closed in, his tenants were harshly treated, farmsteads sold under those who could not pay rent, but his generosity should not be forgotten. He not only gave land in Lancaster for a Girls' School, but at the first meeting impulsively cast 100 guineas on the board.

As the old cottages disappeared there was in 1901, when the population numbered 464, a shortage of housing for the young. Seventy years earlier 872 was the figure. Tarnbrook's 20 dwellings shrank to 2 cottages and 2 farms. It is marvellous to think that some families have farmed in Wyresdale for 400 years. The chance to talk to its people was a privilege and it is to them that I dedicate my little book.

Catherine Rothwell

Waggoners with teams of strong horses to pull the heavy loads were used last century in Wyresdale on the more level lanes and byeways. In such country districts belief persisted that a "horse whisperer" was a carter or waggoner who could control his horses by use of a secret language. The road from Lancashire to Yorkshire via the Trough of Bowland was used by carriers and one of the farms converted to an inn, the Cawthorne Arms, the only one in a parish of 12 townships. J Fenton Cawthorne's land improvements, 3,000 acres in Marshaw and a further 500 acres, resulted in previously worthless moorland reaching a value of 25 shillings an acre.

The waggoner would enjoy his "penny pot of ale", as common in his day as our cup of tea. With Quaker and Wesleyan influence there was little drunkenness; indeed a Band of Hope Temperance Society was formed, but some parishioners accused the beaters attending the shoots on the moors of having their "bottle sups".

Scorton probably earned the term "metropolis" in the 19th. century because it stood on the London, Midland and Scottish Railway main line to the North, but the station is now closed. Long before railways the mail coaches called on their way from London to Scotland. Tolls were payable at Turnpike Gates on the approach to Scorton, charges being laid down by Local Act, e.g. "for every horse, mule or other beast drawing any Coach, Berlin, Landau, Barouche, Gig, Curricle etc. fourpence halfpenny...for every score of Oxen, Cows or neat Cattle the sum of fourpence." The postcard from the 1940s shows the War Memorial at Scorton honouring men from two world wars who paid the highest toll of all.

A letter sent to me from Wyresdale in 1979 by Mr. Frank Williams who stayed at the cottage on the left refers to "the postman in the photograph—he had to walk twenty miles each day delivering letters to the farms. I think his wage at the time was thirty shillings weekly. He died about twenty years ago." At one time letters for Wyresdale were sent to the inns at Lancaster for collection. In the 1940s the children called at Abbeystead Post Office after school and delivered whatever they could on the way home. Once the home of the Drinkalls, it was a distinguished-looking post office built of stone with the date 1677 above the door.

Mary Nichol married Samuel Packard at Calder Bridge in 1855. Both were Wyresdale Quakers. There have been meetings in Wyresdale of the Society of Friends since 1680. Oliver Heywood's Diary of seven years later reports: "Godly dissenters have gained and grown more numerous than ever so that at Chippin, Wyresdale, Poolton meetings... set up where never before." The Pyes and the Kelsalls belonged to the Friends, John Pye from Fellside never questioning the Established Church, but the Craggs, especially Timothy, claimed Quakerism as a phenomenal success breaking new ground in a country district where many had never been baptised or confirmed. Elizabeth Cragg, sister of Timothy, married John Kelsall and it was her mother Jennet of Routen Brook who rode to London on Horseback to rescue her two grandsons, who later attended Abbeystead School. A Meeting House was built in 1883 at a cost of £1,300. In December 1888 there is record of a Quakeress, Mrs. Fanny Brierley, attaining her 100th. year.

Wyresdale men, women and children had to do a lot of walking. John Gorrill and J. Stewardson of Lancaster supplied boots, shoes and leggings, both claiming they had the largest, cheapest and best stocks in the North of England. Stewardson had a sign of a Golden Boot over his premises; Gorrill's one-upmanship was in elastic-sided and Brown Sea Boots, the latter supplied at 2s.–6d. per pair.

Great, great grandmother Catherine Houghton, seated right in the photograph and enjoying a picnic with her family, did her shopping in Lancaster. She was descended from the Garnetts of Wyresdale and was born in the early 1850s. Her eldest son stands beside her, holding the kettle. Her husband died when he was barely forty.

Ainspool, a stream at Ainspool Lane, Kirkland is a Celtic name derived from Abhain, meaning water. In the Amounderness Regional Report of 1937 Churchtown, situated in Kirkland parish, was reckoned as 975 acres. It is the site of one of the most ancient churches in Lancashire. The old photograph shows thatched cottages on the right, the Punch Bowl Hotel on the left and St. Helen's, which was once the parish church for Garstang, at the end of the cobbled street which has no pavements. A new Free School was built at Churchtown in 1812 and the old school in the churchyard, built in 1602, fell into ruins.

Tarnbrook, viewed from Greenside Hill in the early 1900s, now has only three or four dwellings and barns. Here at one time there lived a busy community of Quakers who made gloves and felt top hats. In this cul de sac hamlet, Gornall's Farm, dated 1736, the home of Thomas who ran the Sunday Schools, boys in one cottage, girls in another, was once an inn, The Cross Keys. In the 19th. century when Mary and Billy Simpson lived in the last cottage, dated 1677, numbers even warranted a "Dame School".

The hamlet has inspired a montage displayed in a housing development in the heart of London on the Duke of Westminster's land and named Tarnbrook Court. Dolphinholme Mill's transformation into flats, and Rivers View Fold, "superior cottages", are also modern applications of the local history of Wyresdale.

Oakenclough, where the Parkinson family settled in the 16th. century, was formerly a vaccary of the ancient Forest of Bleasdale. As it was situated in a ravine the waters of the Calder obviously influenced the establishment of a community. Paper mills were set up here in 1774 close to the village of Calder Vale in the township of Barnacre with Bonds. Oakenclough Fold is nearby and an old hostelry, the Moorcock Inn, on the moorland road. In 1820 John Jackson acquired Oakenclough Paper Mill, one of the oldest in the country. By the late 19th. century visitors were making trips to the inns and the valleys such as Nicky Nook, Scorton and Oakenclough. This charabanc party dates from the early 1920s.

Lancaster is linked with Mr. Fenton Cawthorne who had a house there. This view of Market Street from the 1870s shows the Fenton Cawthorne house on the right, which was demolished in 1921, and next door the 1625 King's Arms Hotel, demolished 1880. King's Arms Family and Commercial Hotel Company was its full name and can clearly be seen on the gable end. In 1865 Joseph Sly was proprietor of this inn made famous by Charles Dickens. A bill for that year itemises: "September 7th., Charabanc from Quernmore Park to Bleasdale and back to Quernmore, £1-10-0d" Smith Bretherton and Company ran in 1803 "the only coach to London from the King's Arms, fare—inside 2 guineas; outside £1-6-0d." Mr. Cawthorne, M.P. for Lancaster, also had a house in London where he died, aged 79.

Before the building of the original Roman Catholic Chapel at Scorton, a small thatched dwelling served. Priests used to say Mass in a house called Brackenlea in Nether Wyresdale. In the time of persecution when Mass had to be held in secret it is possible that service was occasionally held at Foxhouses, a dwelling 1½ miles from Scorton because a priest's hiding place has been found there. The church in the photograph was built in 1861. A tablet inside commemorates the work of the Reverend Robert Turpin, "pastor for 25 years and first Mission Rector of this Church" who died February 27th. 1863. Brackenlea is not forgotten: "In 1713 from his home at Brackenlea, Reverend Christopher Jenkinson undertook the charge of the Garstang and Wyresdale Union." In 1963 the priest and people of St. Mary and St. James, Scorton, erected a memorial: "Grateful to God for 250 years of the Holy Sacrament." A small altar in the north aisle, presented by Miss Gillow, came from Clifton Hall, Forton.

Admarsh Chapel is unique in that it is the only one in Lancashire dedicated to St. Eadmor. Some associate the name with King Arthur but history relates Eadmor as friend of St. Anselm, Archbishop of Canterbury. The Chapel at Admarsh probably dates from the 12th. century but the earliest record is of 1610, "a chapel in the King's Chase or Forest". During the 17th. century a period of neglect followed but towards the end of that era, Robert and Christopher Parkinson, trustees of George Piggott, were left £30 to provide a minister for Admarsh in Bleasdale. The Reverend Joseph Stuart, appointed in 1778, preached, and taught for 47 years in the little school attached. The Parkinsons also left money for repairs.

Wyresdale tower in ancient Marshaw vaccary where once dwelt a community of cowherds or neatherds as they were then called, was built by Fenton Cawthorne as an ambitiously-styled shooting lodge but after thirty years it fell into rack and ruin as his high expenditure put an end to some projects. Henry Garnett pulled it down in the 1870s, carting off the valuable stone for Abbeystead House, Brow House and the vicarage at Dolphinholme. The most interesting item remaining is the large stone, once over the doorway of the embattled tower. Standing on the doorstep of Brow House and looking down reveals the inscription on the cartouche now nearly 200 years old:
"This Tower shall live in song and Wyresdale is its name.
John Fenton Cawthorne 1802."

By the late 19th. century traditional ploughing had been abandoned in Wyresdale and steam had killed the water-powered factories and mills. The tenantry under the Earl of Sefton were ordered to kill all rabbits on sight but they were allowed one month of the year in which to snare them, a welcome privilege spelling extra food and money towards their rent. With the advent of motor transport the smithies were less busy. In the 1850s there were two blacksmiths in Over Wyresdale. This photograph of the blacksmith busy shoeing a horse would once be a daily sight. At Higher Lee House a collection of horse-shoes large and small bears witness.

Some indications of an iron mine in Nether Wyresdale have come to light and an old pit in Ridding Wood at the bottom of Chapel House fields. A large heap of iron smelting debris was found on the estate of Captain Ormrod, probably the "Cal-veley" iron mine referred to in the 13th. century. Roger Garnett who died in 1252 had to face an enquiry, having had "a forge raised in the Forest", his share of the iron being nine shillings yearly. Most of the lime kilns were at Sykes in the Trough of Bowland. Old Wyresdale was more industrial with more occupations and there was even a proposal to bring the London and North Western Railway to Tarnbrook.

FAIRY WATERFALL ABBEYSTEAD. Nº 12.

This 1903 photograph of the Fairy Waterfall at Abbeystead is close to where the two sources of the River Wyre meet and is best remembered by older inhabitants as a thrilling spot to reach during school dinner hour in summertime. Abbeystead school was originally endowed by William Cawthorne in 1674 for the benefit of 50 scholars whose parents had to reside in one of the vaccaries. Thomas Richardson, schoolmaster who died in 1793, created a record, holding his post for over 60 years. One hundred and ten yards south of Abbeystead School, earlier Ordnance Survey maps marked "supposed site of abbey". Some believed the 12th. century Cistercian order of friars who moved in 1188 to Wythney in Ireland, built their monastery here, but there is no proof.

This interesting photograph shows workmen in 1903 cutting ice on Abbeystead Reservoir for use in the Ice House at the Mansion. Victorian house parties with huge amounts of food involved made great use of ice in elaborate puddings such as Strawberry Bombe. In the background of the photograph is the gamekeeper's cottage known as Crag House. Abbeystead House was referred to at one time as a palatial shooting box. Hidden from every point except south, it took two years to build and cost £100,000. In 1907 the Earl and Countess of Sefton had an African Sporting Expedition, bringing back to Abbeystead House trophies which included a 13ft. crocodile and a lion, both shot by the Countess.

This fine landau was used for weddings and funerals in Wyresdale district, where a "pyat" or solitary magpie was an evil omen, but in company had significance:

One for sorrow, two for mirth,
Three for a wedding, four for a birth.

In the early 1900s Wyresdale weddings made old-time customs part of the ceremony. A wedding ring placed in a "posset" or mealy drink was poured into cups and shared amongst the unmarried. The person whose cup contained the ring would be the next of the company to marry. Likewise, a large, flat cake of flour, water and currants was baked, containing a wedding ring and a sixpence. When the whole company was about to leave for home after the wedding festivities the cake was broken and distributed amongst the unmarried women. She who found the ring in her portion would shortly be married, but the one who got the sixpence would die an old maid. Weddings averaged 40 guests, well dressed the ladies in tulle picture hats, white silk and feathers. Amongst the wedding gifts for the bride might be a "circular yoke of lace" hand-made such as was presented at Miss Whalley's wedding on July 19th. 1904.

Photographed some years ago is Higher Brock Bridge over the River Brock not far from the once white-fronted, substantial stone dwelling of Brookhouse where it is thought that John Wesley stayed one night on his way north in April 1765. Since the days of the Greenhalgh family the Salisburys and Cunliffes lived there and also, for six years. A. Hewitson, historian and topographer. By 1905 Mr. Isaac Simpson, gold thread manufacturer of Preston, was the occupier. Badgers (broc is the Anglo-Saxon word) bred along the river in olden times as did otters, but both species have now disappeared, although foxes are becoming more numerous. The name Brock recurs in Brock Bottom, a favourite picnic spot; Brock Mill Lane, Claughton; Brock Rakes, Bleasdale, a highway across a gully.

The old, stone-mullioned Beaters' Room at Marshaw still bears the date 1677 when Mr. Hathornthwaite lived there. Members of his family resided at the vaccary of their namesake and also at Marshaw, Tarnbrook, Lea and Catshaw. This building passed down to landowner Fenton Cawthorne who utilised it as an inn, the Cawthorne Arms. Under the Seftons it became a gamekeeper's house, "Keeper's Cottage", where hearty meals were eaten when the shooting parties came down from the moors. The beaters' job was to flush out the grouse and pheasants so that the gentry could shoot the birds in flight. The Earl of Sefton added the smaller, newer building on the left, around the walls of which were photographs of past shooting parties. George V. dined here in 1926.

Waterworks buildings and entrance to Abbeystead reservoir, now presided over by North West Water, can be seen in this photograph from 1965. Water from the gathering grounds in the hills near Lancaster was harnessed to power mills along the River Wyre, but with the advent of steam this became unnecessary. Nearby, the grounds of the Home Farm to the Mansion, stacked with much Bowland forest timber, lead to the site of the Abbeystead Water Scheme, scene of the tragedy on May 23rd. 1984 when 16 people died, amongst them Geoffrey, husband of the late celebrated Pat Seed. A brass plaque in St. Michael's Church commemorates this terrible event, litigation from which was not resolved until 1989. Trained nurse and farmer's wife Tizzie Entwistle of Lentworth Farm heard the explosion as her family were playing tennis that early evening. First on the scene, Mrs. Entwistle indeed put her nursing skills to the test.

"The Country Postman", painted by G. L. Seymour in 1884 must have looked like this coming into Scorton, Abbeystead and Ortner. Found in an old newspaper also in Wyresdale was an interesting report from the Theatre Royal, Covent Garden, when famous actor Mr. Kemble was appearing on the very night, October 21st. 1805. "The news of Admiral Nelson's victory produced a burst of patriotic exultation rarely witnessed in a theatre. Rule Britannia was lustily called for, then a second time sung. The acclamations were the loudest and most fervent we have ever witnessed." After the play, "Venice Preserved", a loyal music impromptu, "Nelson's Glory", was given.

The deeply wooded area of Ortner in Over Wyresdale is fed by innumerable streams and minor tributaries of the Wyre. Because of its isolated position shut away from most eyes it was probably chosen by the Quakers escaping from religious persecution, a similar area to the one they found at Briggflatts, Sedbergh.

This photograph from twenty years ago shows the well-wooded area round Abbeystead House, land which was purchased by the Seftons from Henry Garnett of Wyreside, another mansion situated at Dolphinholme. In 1897 Lady Rose Mary Molyneux (the family name of the Seftons) was left an allowance of £5,000 to maintain Abbeystead House. Since the estate was purchased by its present owner, the Duke of Westminster, Christmas parties have been held for Estate tenants and workers and on rare occasions part of the house opened to the public.

The Seftons attended Wyresdale Church where an old cello hung on the vestry wall, a relic from the days when there was no organ. Instrumentalists on double bass, serpent, bassoon, led the choir and the congregation turned to "face the music". This links with harvest festivals and old-style haymaking when gangs of men using long-bladed scythes mowed the meadows, to be followed by the tedders with their hay forks forming haycocks and stacks.

The photograph shows the entrance to Wyresdale Park, Scorton, now much changed, but in its day a costly residence built for £50,000. Surrounded by woods north east of Scorton village, this towered structure was the home of Mr. Peter Ormrod, wealthy head of a Bolton banking firm, Hardcastle, Cross and Company. Commenced in 1856, it was not completed until 1865. A nephew, Colonel Cross Ormrod, lived there and his son Captain Peter Ormrod eventually inherited the property. The Captain brought a herd of fallow deer to Scorton, releasing them in the Park. He also built up a famed pack of staghounds, the opening day of the Hunt being November 8th. 1899. Hare coursing was another of his favoured sports.

A photograph from the 1930s of Brock station in the heart of a rural community. Not far away are two ornamental bridges bearing the badger emblem of the Fitzherbert Brockholes family of Claughton Hall. The Squire had not wanted a railway to pass through his land at all, but eventually agreeing, he stipulated that the bridges must be architecturally pleasing. Approaching is a "Royal Scot" class locomotive. Signal box, Crossing and Lancaster and Preston stone station building are signs of the past. The wooden structure marked "Parcel Office and Cloak Room" was added later by the Lancashire and North Western Railway. Never a busy station, it had to close in 1939.

The great, lonely tracts of Bleasdale and Wyresdale have been used by the Government in two world wars. Although access has now been allowed to seven and a half miles of what has hitherto been private land beyond Tarnbrook, a warning notice to keep to paths and beware of unexploded shells is still displayed at the gate leading to Gilberton. During World War 11 Tarnbrook Fell became a battle-training ground and live ammunition was used. The photograph shows military training in the Wyresdale area from the days of World War 1. Corporal Smith, third from the left, came from Kirkby Lonsdale. In June 1804 the Lancaster Volunteers "had a field day" brigading under Lieutenant Colonels Bradshaw and Grimshaw.

Some members of the public clamour for greater access, but many walkers causing erosion would mar this area of outstanding natural beauty and there is always the fear of peat and heather catching fire. In 1946 wide areas of Tarnbrook Fell were burned as fires swept over moorland.

22

In the 1860s Garstang farmers found progress to market was slow and difficult along the narrow, winding lanes. This was why a railway was proposed which would link Over-Wyre with Garstang and thus on to Preston. Wilson France, the Squire of Rawcliffe, was the chief proposer, his agent John Addis canvassing local leading men. In December 1863 a Prospectus was issued, the six directors being James Bourne, Richard Bennett, John Russell, James Overend, Julian Tarner and Henry Gardner. Galbraith and Tolme of London were the Company's Engineers, but by April 1865 only half a mile of the bed of the proposed railway track had been prepared, the first contractor, Wheatley Kirk, resigning over money matters.

Today Garstang is a shopping town for the country around including Wyresdale and after centuries of commerce the Thursday Market, upon which all local producers base their prices, still continues. The canal, now a pleasant waterway for leisure craft, greatly helped trade.

In 1784 when he was 25 travelling preacher Michael Emmett first visited Wyresdale and was favourably received when he preached to the shepherds. Two years later he married Mary, sister of Roger Crane, all being devout Methodists. In later life Mary put up John Wesley at her house on his last visit through Lancaster. A wealthy friend having supplied a horse, Emmett set off from Preston, preaching first in Garstang before moving on to Scorton and Upper Wyresdale. At Garstang a Quaker gave him a guinea at the end of his sermon, which Michael at first refused, but the kindly Mr. Jackson pointed out, "Thou cannot pay thy toll bars and keep thy horse without money. Keep it lad and go on with the work thou hast so well begun." The old Wesleyan Chapel built at Higher Emmetts was on land given by Lawrence Pye but the chapel in the photograph is nearer Lea on a site given by the Earl of Sefton, the old chapel now being part of Emmetts Farm.

Calder Vale Church, built by public subscription, stands between Calder Vale and Oakenclough in a very picturesque area and is here photographed ten years ago by Stanley Butterworth. Dedicated to St. John the Evangelist and consecrated on August 12th. 1863, the church contains a fine Caen stone pulpit in memory of W. J. Garnett of Quernmore Park who gave the site. The formation of the Fylde Waterworks Company in 1860 led to the construction of reservoirs, one at Sullam, a mile from Calder Vale Church, where Squire Tyldesley used to go "a fox hunting" 1712—14, where once wild deer roamed and on whose summit an annual fair was held for the sale of gingerbread and toys from time immemorial. Over the years clear sightings of the Isle of Man were made from Sullam. Surplus water from the lower, less well constructed reservoir ran off into the River Wyre.

Margaret Harrison of Carr House, Garstang, was the daughter of John Townson of Chapel House Wyresdale, and sister of the heroic Quakeress Jennet Cragg who in 1687 rode on horseback from Quernmore to London, returning with her two orphaned grandsons who grew up as Quakers in the Wyreside community, industrious, God-fearing people. Wyreside Quaker records reveal that Gornall's Farm, once an inn, also housed Thomas Gornall, a Quaker who made hats. Glove makers and hatters lived in Tarnbrook hamlet then, for it was a Quaker community of over twenty houses. There was also established by William Gornall of Tarnbrook, Over Wyresdale, a black felt hat making workroom in Forton Board School which finished operation c.1840. Records of the Friends, e.g. the minutes of the Society of Wyresdale Preparative Meeting, can be perused at the Lancashire Record Office. The photograph shows Gornall's Farm with shepherd Jack Pye standing at the door.

Calder House at Calder Bridge was the home of Mary Dilworth and David her brother, the children of John Jackson and Ann Dilworth, who farmed at Ortner in Wyresdale for 27 years. Mary was married in 1855 from Calder House to Jonathan Abbott, shoe maker and Quaker. The love letters they exchanged during their courtship have recently been published in a well researched book about the Quakers of this area. Richard Jackson who died on January 3rd. 1848 is recorded as "a good and faithful servant in the family of the late Thomas Townley of Ortner." Three Jackson brothers left their home in Lower Wyresdale to become manufacturers of paper and cotton in the village of Calder Vale and in 1828 built the Meeting House at Bonds. Calder Bridge Meeting House was well supported. It is said that John Bright, "The Tribune of the People", who attended the old Quaker School at Newton-in-Bowland, carved his name on a wooden form there in 1826. He said the chief things he learned were "to fish, to take wasps' nests and to eat oatcake".

Calder Vale in the early 1900s shows Dodding's General Store at the end of Long Row. From here Mr. Dodding went out with his horse and covered cart to hawk provisions in the surrounding countryside. He was a welcome caller at the farms and cottages as were the tinkers and pedlars with their packs. There is a Tinkers Lane in the area.

In those days "Attock Sunday" was celebrated when the fields were stacked with corn sheaves after the cutting by scythes. Another regular ritual was the sheep washing and shearing which started in June. A dam was placed across the streams to form a pool. As the sheep were released from nearby pens the farmers, standing in water, immersed each one, rubbing its wool. This was done in the early morning so that the wool would dry in time for the "clippers". Tasks completed, it was a time of feast and merriment in which everybody joined including the children, who had helped by holding the sheep's legs so that the shearer was not kicked.

Abbeystead 60 acre reservoir was twice stocked with trout. The Corporation of Lancaster built it to supply mills in dry seasons so that domestic supplies would not suffer. Streams brought down earth and stones which sedimented into the reservoir and caused problems. Constructed in 1853 to hold 28½ million gallons of water, it was enlarged in 1865 to hold 76½ million gallons when William Roper was Chairman of the Water Committee. Further enlargement and reconstruction in 1881 increased capacity to 185 million gallons. However, much of the power went to waste when the fitting of steam engines made the old water wheels redundant.

Old residents remembered how the water rushed down nightly from the huge dam, giving enough power to reach the down-river corn mill of Garstang and Corless mill, Dolphinholme. The photograph shows the salmon ladder, part of the reservoir complex.

The ancient Forest of Wyresdale adjoined those of Bleasdale and Quernmore. Hunting rights belonged to the king and people who lived in the confines were subject to special laws, the Court of the Forest being known as the Woodmote. At about the time of Henry V11 the vaccaries were let to tenants and then began the building of the stone homesteads. An early family to settle were the Parkinsons, Thomas obtaining the vaccary of Swainshead early in Queen Elizabeth's reign. The Thomas Parkinson who settled in Wyresdale from Bleasdale erected a mill without that Queen's permission and was summoned to the Woodmote in 1601. Poaching of deer was harshly punished. Wolf Fell indicates that wolves did roam and there was a wolf house built as a place of refuge. A relic from this, a massive oak door studded with knobs, was discovered many years ago. Another much later relic is this old grindstone.

The photograph by Stanley Butterworth shows Bleasdale Circle in summer some twenty years ago. First described in 1899, it actually consists of two circles one inside the other and a third innermost shaped like a horse shoe. In the centre were two cinerary urns containing human ashes, suggesting that Bronze Age men buried their dead here. When the original wooden posts were removed to the Harris Museum in Preston it was found that well below ground they were still whole. Their positions are now marked by concrete blocks. Looking towards Fairsnape there is a commanding view of hills and plain. From behind, the ridge of Blindhurst Fell dominates, a mysterious and well-chosen place to set the imagination racing and roving back to the days of wolves, wild boars and primitive men dressed in animal skins.

STATION LANE. SCORTON.

Before the motorway was made the steep road out of Scorton led to bracken-clad banks where curlews nested. On the left could be seen Wyresdale Park with its lake. For many years the scene had never changed. In this photograph Station Lane leading to Scorton Mill shows the three-storey, stone-built houses in which mill operatives probably lived. There can also be seen an older dwelling, its thatched roof replaced with corrugated iron or some substitute. Much of the property in Nether Wyresdale, including the village of Scorton, belonged to the Duke of Hamilton. When the Duke's property was sold, 4,027 acres in Nether Wyresdale were purchased by Peter Ormrod, head of a banking firm from Bolton, with the intention of improving the area. Wyresdale Park was commenced in 1856 but the substantial structure with its tower was not completed until 1865. Hundreds of acres were also purchased in Cabus and Cleveley.

A lawsuit in 1622 stated that the tithe barn and tithe corn of Scorton were let at £43 a year, but what was once termed "the metropolis of Wyresdale" is not an ancient place. The earliest reference I found was 1587. There was no school until 1793 when the Duke of Hamilton provided land and the villagers money. The present Roman Catholic Church up Snow Hill replaced a tiny thatched building used as church on Sunday and clogger's shop during the week. Scorton was once unique in having neither public house, doctor nor village policeman. In the 1950s the population of Nether Wyresdale was 600 but always at weekends this was augmented by walkers and cyclists in search of the famous home-made ice cream. A special bus on Thursdays took villagers to Garstang Market.

The photograph shows the barn of Springfield Farm. Mr. George Fishwick owned farm, mill and the big house Springfield. The original farmhouse was across the road and is now called "Kettlewell", the residence of Mr. Richmond.

An early mention of "Scurton" was made in a will dated 1587. An 1872 list of Scorton's attractions mentions: a good brass band; one of the best tenors in the realm, Mr. W. Parkinson; a public clock; a maypole; a church and chapel and a cotton factory. Preesall Brass Band, photographed here, played in this area in the 1900s. The Maypole, erected near the big house, Springfield, was last seen in the 1900s rotting away and "the whale's jawbone, put up like an arch", seems to have vanished. It was reputed that John Wesley preached under the old oak tree or "stone tree" in front of the Methodist Chapel, the stone referring to a stone seat which once encircled the oak but which was damaged and finally despatched by the coming of the motor age. For 300 years the Sandwell family lived at Scorton Hall. A descendant of this family ran a small beer shop in 1830 as Scorton had no inn, but it had to close.

GATHERING BLUEBELLS
BROCK.

Posed by a travelling photographer, the boy and girl are gathering bluebells in Brock, from time immemorial a recognised, well-wooded beauty spot which used to be called "an earthly paradise of sylvan beauty". Paradise Woods and Paradise Cottage which became Paradise Farm are names stemming from this description. Various branches of the Parkinson family have lived in the district, there being a William Parkinson of Brockside whose will was proved at Lancaster in 1729. Brock Bottom could at one time be reached from Brock station. A lane led to the dismantled mill with its row of cottages dating back to the days of the Industrial Revolution. Water was used also to turn the wheel of a corn mill situated at Lower Brock Bridge. It is possible that this old photograph from c.1902 is of Paradise Woods with the steep ravine known as Vale of Paradise on the opposite side.

The Estate Office in Abbeystead is the nerve centre of the 4th. Duke of Westminster's Grosvenor Estate i.e. that part appertaining to Abbeystead. To maintain the 19,500 acres of which 13,000 are moorland and 6,000 tenanted requires foresters, gamekeepers, rangers, farmers and dry-stone wallers. The photograph from the 1980s shows a typical Marshaw dry-stone wall repaired by local boy Andrew Curwen. His Grace, who purchased the Estate in December 1980 from the executors of the Seftons, feels a strong obligation to nature conservancy and has invested in moorland recovery. Roads and tracks over the fells, rebuilding of follies such as the Gad House between Abbeystead and Lower Lee, and a 25-year plan for the felling and replacement of woodlands are involved. In the days of the big grouse shooting parties held by the sporting Duke, Hugh William Osbert Molyneux, 7th. Earl of Sefton, born 1895, Littledale held the world record in 1915.

This ancient rotary quern was discovered at the Church of St. Helen in 1939. Sometimes used as baptismal fonts, their primary function was for the pounding of wheat in order to separate the husks from the flour which, once obtained, was baked into clap bread by the addition of water. This quern could have originated in Tarnbrook where it is known that next to the smithy, stone delphs were worked.

Wyresdale farms were supplied with kists for storing oatmeal-covered sides of bacon, and the daintier spice cupboards let into the wall by the fireplace, usually dated by a wood carver.

Lentworth corn mill, seen in this photograph, is mentioned in documents from 1601. In the 17th. century the Leeming family had charge. Perhaps it was one of their descendants who has roughly carved the date in the outer walls. The great apple-wood wheel turned for the last time in the 1850s. There were many such mills along the river banks, powered by water from the Wyre and Calder. In 1610 Dunkenshaw mill was leased to John Bond but there were millers of this name long before then.

The photograph shows the beautiful, ancient tower of the Church of St. Michael. In November 1956 during repairs to the church, remains of an early 14th. century painting of the Ascension came to light on the north wall of the Sanctuary. Six hundred years ago when most people could not read, church walls were illustrated in order to teach the Scriptures. Accounts show that the bell ringers and choristers of centuries ago were paid with a flagon of ale. In 1681 payment was also made by the churchwardens for pests such as magpies (one penny for each head). Place names around indicate the presence of Saxons and Danes. In the 1890s a cinerary urn was found at Crossmoor, Wyresdale with the remains of sword and dagger close by. There is a bell dated 1458 and a 13th. century pedestal for the vanished statue of Saint Michael which like that of Saint Helen from Churchtown was probably thrown into the River Wyre by Cromwell's despoiling soldiery.

The monks of Wyresdale arranged for a chaplain at St. Michael's who had fishing rights near the church granted to him and "half a mark of silver yearly" but they required the chapel to pay the tithe of corn, fish and cattle and reserved the right to erect a mill on St. Michael's church land, the chaplain not to claim multure.

Shireshead Old Church, thought to have been in existence in 1520, stood on high ground at Cleveley not far from the River Wyre. Recusant fines of £40 paid by Roman Catholic John Bradshaw went towards the upkeep of a minister to serve at the church in 1646. Reconstructed in 1805, it was supported by Scorton C. of E. members in the 1840s. Mr. and Mrs. Henry Garnett of Wyresdale attended for many years with their nine sons and three daughters. In 1878, St. Peter's church and vicarage were built at the south end of Scorton village, the cost of £13,000 being met by Peter Ormrod's brother.

Half a mile away at Hollins Lane there used to be a small community of poverty-stricken rag gatherers and hawkers. Their neglected children were instructed every Sunday by George Fishwick who, when winter came, had a small preaching house installed. He "went with his dinner in his pocket and toiled all day."

Gornall's Farm, Tarnbrook, dated 1730 W.G.I. is here photographed in the 1920s. The trees are no longer there. Behind Gornall's, high on the fell side is the ancient farm of Gilbertson, written Gilbertholme in old documents, a lonely fertile place by the gill of Spreight Clough. Pony tracks used to lead to sheds, luncheon huts and shooting butts where the great grouse shoots were held and where for convenience lunch could be eaten instead of returning to Abbeystead House. One record "bag" of grouse numbered 2,929.

Another view of the 1887 Lodge leading to Abbeystead House. At the death of the 6th. Earl in 1897 the property was left to his favourite daughter Rose Mary who lived on there until her death. She loved Abbeystead and took great interest in the tenants and in Wyresdale. Embowered in trees, both Lodge and Mansion reflect the on-going work of close attention to woodland. By his enthusiasm and encouragement, the 4th. Duke of Westminster, acknowledged to be a good landlord and employer, has given reassurance to anyone who might have been apprehensive about change.

The corn mill built by Anthony Richardson in 1548 must have been the original Brock Mill. As it was newly established, Ralph Parkinson had refused to acknowledge the owner's right of soke, so he was refused the right to grind his corn there. The subsequent lawsuit seems to have continued in the Duchy Court on and off for thirty years.

The young man in the photograph is thought to be a descendant of Richard Hall of Pilling who followed the course of the River Wrye from its sources to the sea and wrote a poem of 32 verses which was printed in 1882. Of Brock Mill he wrote:

"A structure of capacious size
And with machinery lined.
Upon the river's bank there stood
Both corn and grain to grind.
For some few yards the water fell
Upon a tumbling wheel
That groaned beneath the river's might
To drive the grinding steel."

Hall's had a chemist's shop in Lancaster.

Wesleyan Methodism flourished in Over Wyresdale at the beginning of the 19th. century although the pioneers had much opposition from the Established Church. Jenny Cornall, an employee at the Scorton cotton mill, who held services in her cottage, was annoyed by villagers placing sods on her chimney but eventually her devotion to the cause triumphed. After hearing him at Scorton and Garstang an Over Wyre farmer asked the landlord's son from the Ram's Head in Preston to preach. Members of the Wyresdale Society of Methodists in 1803 were: Grace and Christopher Gates; J. Bibby; William and Richard Winder; Mary and Isa Bibby; Thomas Gornall; John and Ann Dodding. Dr. Newton, introduced by Mr. Fishwick of Scorton, was one of the most popular preachers. John Bibby of Well Brook Farm was known as the Marquis because of his aristocratic appearance and calm, pious temperament. The building of this Methodist Chapel in 1842 on a site supplied by the Duke of Hamilton was paid for by George Fishwick of Scorton who died at the age of 65. His daughter Mary, also a devout Methodist, was very attached to the people of Scorton and greatly missed at her early death.

Dolphinholme may well have been the first place in the country to be lighted by gas, installed in 1801 chiefly to serve the worsted woollen mill in the village, which in its heyday employed 1,400 workers. The lamp in the photograph, the last of the original fittings, was formerly at the end of the row, Corless Cottages in Higher Dolphinholme, but has been restored and fixed onto the corner of Derham House. Raw material was supplied by the factory to the cottages and farms as far away as Forton, Galgate and Wyresdale for combing and carding. Carding instruments have been found at farms and Mr. W. Winder, church clerk, had a chest of drawers made out of a weaving machine which had been used by one of his relatives.

The mill weir at Dolphinholme, a requisite of primitive corn mills, was reported in a 16th. century document as the highest up the River Wyre. Others noted were Corless Mill, Cleveley Mill and "a mill near Goberthwaite Bridge". Dolphinholme Mill closed in 1867 and population shrank to 400 by the end of the century. There is still a wagon road along which supplies for the mill came from Bradford on horse-drawn carts. The workforce helped to push the heavy wagons up the hill.

A report on wayside crosses in the Garstang area over half a century ago reveals ten in various states, e.g. Hagwood Cross, Mony Pads, Brunahill, Cathouses. In 1902 a 3ft. high cross was still in Mr. Curwen's garden at Bowgreave, about half a mile from Garstang Market Place. Most unusual, there was a complete stone cross reported in 1848 half a mile east of Claughton Hall on the road skirting Claughton Park.

It was customary to rest the corpse in its coffin by these wayside crosses on the way to the church of St. Helen and pray. Thomas Bell of Garstang was carried this way. "People assisted to carry the corps of T.B. deceased and same was set down at crosses using such superstitious solemnity and interring the same corps without minister or prayers." Those at fault had to confess before the bishop, take communion and promise never to do so again. The cross in the photograph is at Claughton.

The photograph of White Moor dates from c.1900, the farm worker in the foreground probably being David Ritchie. The outbuilding alongside the dry-stone wall was evidently once covered with thatch of long standing, showing the typical 18th. century framework for such. During the second world war there was a Searchlight Unit stationed at this point. White Moor Farm, which was pulled down many years ago, was situated close to Wyresdale Tower.

Although some may have been inserted at a later date into more recent buildings, datestones, linked to further research, can give information about ownership of other old farms in the area. Reverend Daniel Schofield reported that the oldest stone was in the west gate of Lentworth Barn when the Claytons were tenants. Thomas and Mary Drinkel, of the Drinkall family who have farmed for 400 years, inscribed theirs in 1662: "Whoever looks upon this thing, let him fear God and honour the King."

Of the twenty Wyresdale vaccaries or pastures for cows which are recorded in 1324 some later disappeared or merged, reducing the number to twelve. Indentures show that Marshaw, Hathornthwaite, Dunkenshaw and Abbeystead became the property of William Cawthorne. In 1821 John Fenton Cawthorne enclosed and drained land, dividing open moorland by stone walls six feet high into fields from 15 to 60 acres in size. 85 loads of lime to the acre caused ling to disappear and grass to grow, which could support cattle. On higher, rocky land he planted trees which later rooted well elsewhere. By 1852 Robert and William Garnett were owners of the Royal Forests of Bleasdale, Quernmore and Wyresdale. Strong farm buildings featured gateposts (stoops) and walls like those in the photograph at Greenlands Farm, Claughton-on-Brock which can still be found throughout the vaccaries. A pinfold gate and stoops could be supplied for ten shillings in 1797.

Inside Wyresdale Chapel many years ago when oil lamps were in use. The oldest date, 1684, is on the pulpit. Later church buildings probably used some of the old materials from the one being replaced. It is thought that three arches inside Higher Lea House may have come from an earlier chapel. In its long history there must have been a number of rebuildings, one of which took place in 1733. "...building the steeple 22 September 1733 £1,245." The last restoration was done by Philip, 4th. Earl of Sefton, after he completed the building of Abbeystead House. Plaster was removed from walls; new font, vestry, chancel, organ and oak benches installed. Until 1860 the pews were carpeted with rushes.

The ancient land system within Wyresdale, originally one large vaccary or cow pasture, dates from Norman times. In 1324 vaccaries were named as follows, some being recognised today: Swainshead; Catshew; Groghbrook; Hawthornthwaite; Hindshaw; Marshaw; Over Gilbertholme; Dunkinshaw; Mickle Lea; Little Lea; Emmets; Abbeystead; White Ridding; Lentworth; Cleveley; Ortner; Hare Appletree; Routen Brook and Tarnbrook. By the 1820s Mr. Weld of Stonyhurst owned the vaccary of Lentworth; Mr. Clarkson, Emmots, described as "well cultivated". The vaccary of Ortner was completely enclosed but there was no outpasture. Tarnbrook had extensive pasturage but little enclosed land. However, there was a useful quarry of freestone, slates and flags. The old photograph of Brow House shows part of the vaccary of Abbeystead.

The oak, carved cupboard at Gornall's Farm, Tarnbrook, photographed some years ago, is dated 1678 G.I.E., a date older than that outside the farm itself, 1730 W.G.I. Higher Lea Farm, dated 1671 R.W.P., was doubtless built and lived in by the Parkinson family. Lancaster Cottage, Tarnbrook, later used as a shippon, may also have been associated with the Parkinsons as it bore a 1677 datestone initialled C.E.P. The inscription 1677 N.E.D. T.D. at Abbeystead Post Office refers to Nicholas Drinkall who is listed in old documents as one of the five tenants of Abbeystead vaccary under the Duchy of Lancaster.

This bobbin mill near Scorton, photographed in the 1940s, was one of a number powered by the waters of the River Wyre or Calder. Bobbins were used in the cotton and silk mills. In the days of the Gardners, five generations of them, timber was stacked in the big yard of this mill and salmon caught in the sluice, where the torrent from Harrisend Fell was dammed. When released, this force of water drove the great wheel. There were silk mills at the foot of the valley near Scorton and cotton mills at Galgate. "Cart loads of bobbins went to Gawgat," said John Cookson of Stonehead Farm. Besides bobbins the mill also made door "snecks" or latches. The Gardners had a millstone grit quern like the one illustrated on another page, which came from Bracken Lea and may have been used for Catholic baptism.

The cotton mill, now in ruinous state, was built early in the 19th. century, using water power for spinning. Sluices, dam, weir and the mill itself are now of great interest to the industrial archaeologist. Supposedly the first of the compound kind in Lancashire as it eliminated the traditional hand and foot operations, it was not entirely a success. It passed down to George Fishwick who lived in Scorton until his death in 1854 and built the Methodist Chapel shown in another photograph. Most of the mill, originally three storeys high, was pulled down by Colonel Cross Ormrod and by the early 1900s it was being used as a joiner's shop.

HIGH STREET. GARSTANG.

The photograph of High Street, Garstang from the late 1920s reminded one old inhabitant of Wyresdale of the hiring fair which took place at Garstang around Martinmas, November 11th. "Most of the crops were in, Harvest Homes had been held and the old-time farming year was beginning again. At that Garstang Fair thousands of cattle were sold and the hiring of men, boys and lasses took place. From all over the Fylde and Wyresdale hundreds of farming folk flocked for the days of the fair." After the hirings there was more money around so the pedlars and hawkers timed their visits to coincide. Farm workers were paid for the whole year, their food provided. Some farms had a reputation for "keeping a good table" and retaining their workers whilst others had difficulty in recruiting new labour.

The old photograph of Higher Lee shows how this yeoman's house, dating back to the Parkinson family of the 17th. century, looked before Mr. and Mrs. Apedaile made alterations which restored the house to its original state. The road was moved and the projecting outbuildings taken down, ivy stripped from the front of the house to be replaced with rambler roses. Lawns were sown and the area around cultivated with flowers, the setting making use of a natural stream flowing into Grizedale Brook, to form a water garden.

On December 31st. 1717 Christopher Parkinson of Higher Lee and his daughter were crossing from Wardstone to Harterbeck when mist fell. The daughter became so exhausted she died on the moorland. Hatter, John Drinkall narrowly escaped death from exposure and Robert Birkett of Lower Lee lost his life on High Cross Moor. His apprentices, sent to search, found him unconscious but he never recovered.

THE BY-PASS, GARSTANG.

Near here one of the last toll bars was done away with in 1840. A century later at a time of sparse traffic, the figure in the roadway points to one route into Wyresdale. The X.L. Hotel has since become the Chequered Flag. Further along the A6 is the Hamilton Arms which used to be called the Old Holly or Old Hollins, the largest inn between Preston and Lancaster, to which stone marten hunters in Scorton Park came for refreshment. Not far away in Hollins Lane at a smaller inn, the Middle Holly, a group of linen weavers under the charge of Matthew Hall earned a reputation for bullying. The New Holly building appeared in the late 18th. century and to add to confusion there was another New Holly at Forton close to coaching stables. Squire Tyldesley refers to the New Holly in his 18th. Century Diary.

A schedule of tenants in the manor of Nether Wyresdale in 1604 names Barnacre and Bonds as separate townships. The Roman Catholic Church is the building on the right of this 1920s photograph. Boundaries alter with the passing years, causing some confusion. Parkhead Brook, a tributary of the River Wyre, and Lady Hamilton's Well, the spa where members of the Hamilton family went to bathe, were in the confines, Grizedale being the boundary of Nether Wyresdale and Barnacre with Bonds. For 300 years the Turner family farmed at Bonds. Lawrence, who occupied the farm until his death in January 1879, was one of 18 children. A stone relic which belonged to the family was converted into a receptacle for holy water in Bonds Roman Catholic Church. It is dated 1639 and bears the initials R.T. which were also on the stable door at the farm with a corresponding date.

BONDS, GARSTANG.

Abbeystead Lodge "Lancaster" was built on the slopes of Emmots Brow where once was a house belonging to the Clayton family. The Marshaw Wyre flows past the front of the Mansion's garden and into the reservoir, a fine view of which is obtainable from the high ground behind. Above the mullioned window can be seen the interlaced monogram of the Earl's two daughters, Lady Gertrude and Lady Rose Mary. In both Lancaster and York Lodges the carved rose in the stonework is conspicuous. The family motto was "To conquer is to live enough".